Pictorial Memories of
OLD
ABERSYCHAN

including
TALYWAIN, GARNDIFFAITH
and VARTEG

by Bryan Roden
& Malcolm Thomas

Foreword by
The Rt. Hon. Paul Murphy, MP
Secretary of State for Wales

Old Bakehouse Publications

Abertillery

First published in October 1999

ISBN 1 874538 52 2

Published in the U.K. by
Old Bakehouse Publications
Church Street,
Abertillery, Gwent NP13 lEA
Telephone: 01495 212600 Fax: 01495 216222

Made and printed in the UK
by J.R. Davies (Printers) Ltd.

Foreword

by
The Rt. Hon. Paul Murphy, MP
Secretary of State for Wales

I take enormous pleasure in writing the foreword to this excellent book. My family on my father's and mother's sides - lived in Abersychan since the 1860s, and I myself was brought up in 6 Station Street, until moving to Cwmbran in the late 1960s.

I still feel that I am an 'Abersychan boy' and many of my relatives still live in the village. When I was a pupil at West Mon School, I wrote a short history of Abersychan, which, of course, was never published!

This book - by Bryan Roden and Malcolm Thomas - fulfils a great need - to put into print not only a history of Abersychan, Talywain, Garndiffaith and Varteg, but also to provide a unique photographic record of those very special communities.

This is a splendid book - well-written and beautifully illustrated, which will be cherished by all those who have a special place in their hearts for the northern part of our Eastern Valley.

Many of the photographs bring back personal memories - on page 10, reference is made to my maternal grandfather, J.H. Pring; on pages 11 and 14, to the 'Colliers Arms' which was where I lived; on page 60, to the Catholic church where I was confirmed; on page 85, to my grandmother's family - the Goughs - who owned shops in the area; on page 112, to the Llanerch & Blaensychan collieries where my grandfather and father both worked - and so on!

The book is a treasure-house of memories, we all owe Bryan and Malcolm a great debt.

Contents

Introduction

Considerably widespread, the Abersychan Urban District was once the largest in terms of acreage in Monmouthshire, and this book attempts to cover as many corners and aspects as possible. There is an extensive collection of photographs, depicting the scenery and people within that district, over a period of more than a hundred years. As a century closes and a new millennium approaches, it is appropriate that we now focus and reflect a little on the enormous changes that have affected so much. The earliest account of the region appears to be that mentioned in a Bill of Complaint addressed to Thomas, Earl of Suffolk, Lord High Treasurer in the year 1616. The charge was that there had been *'unlawful seizure of certain waste land in the Parish of Trevethin at Abersychan, Gellisychan, the Garn, Tal y Waen and the brook Sychan'.* The name Abersychan is derived from the combination of *Aber* - meaning a confluence of rivers, *Sych* - dry and *An* or *Ain* - brook.

Once a most rural part of the Eastern Valley, with farming as the chief occupation, the mineral and industrial discoveries of the first quarter of the nineteenth century soon transformed the landscape forever. The manufacture of iron and the unearthing of coal, were to become the new mainstays of the local economy and so heralded the establishment of hamlets such as Varteg, Garndiffaith and Talywain, to name but a few. Coal was mined at the Varteg Level from about 1808, thus requiring the building of dwelling places to accommodate the workers; consequently such names as Incline Row, Slate Row and Twenty Houses began to appear, all since demolished but still avid in the memories of a few surviving souls. Adequate housing however, was not seen as a priority by employers or local councils, just as long as the wheels of industry were kept in motion. An extract from a report of 1909 for instance, describes the situation during a visit to Percy Street Garndiffaith. *'Number 20 is exceedingly poor with interior walls boarded up to restrain the damp, and has two adults and four children under the age of seven as its occupants. No.21 has two cases of typhoid. No.29 has four cases, not helped by the outside W.C. which serves seven adults and ten children. No.14 is in mourning, the sole breadwinner having died of the fever at Lasgarn Isolation Hospital this morning'.*

Early ironworks in the vicinity were established at Varteg in 1802, Pentwyn in 1825 and by 1827, the works of Messrs. Small, Shears and Taylor, known as the British Ironworks, were in production. The name 'British' was to lend itself to the area surrounding the works, and so evolved, yet another community within the Abersychan District. The ironworks however, did not share the prosperity and extended life enjoyed by the coal industry, it closing in the early 1880s, whilst coal was mined in the locality for a further one hundred years. There followed a speedy growth in population through the latter half of the nineteenth century, leading to the development of Abersychan town itself. High Street was awash with traders and amenities of all description by the year 1900, difficult to imagine these days perhaps, but the evidence rests in many of the pictures in this book. Essential, and ever-popular Co-operative Stores were to be found all around, moral guidance was upheld in almost twenty places of worship and who could forget such venues as the 'Garn Hall' for moments of pleasure?

For good measure, the book also includes a selection of photographs portraying numerous personalities and the like, who have resided in these parts over the years; a feature that will hopefully prompt a few pleasant recollections from readers young, and old.

Bryan Roden

Malcolm Thomas

CHAPTER 1

Abersychan and the surrounding area

1. This initial photograph from the year 1907 of Snatchwood Road, well-illustrates a number of changes that have affected this part of Abersychan during the twentieth century. The two prominent buildings on the left have these days been converted into private dwellings. In earlier years however, the smaller of the two was a busy local shop whilst the larger was a hostelry known as the Snatchwood Inn. This one-time 'Pub' was purchased for the grand sum of £445 in 1896 by Mr. Charles Westlake, owner of the brewery at Blaenavon and in later years also at Cwmavon. The gentleman on the right of the picture and wearing a bowler hat, stands near the entrance to Longfield House.

2. From the same period as the previous photograph the scene is set a little further up the road. On the right are the well-built bay-fronted houses of Snatchwood Road with some picturesque, but much older cottages on the opposite side. The cottages have since been demolished and the road nowadays is a far cry from this peaceful Edwardian setting.

3. An early view which is taken from behind Pontnewynydd Board Schools. Two features to look for are the distant stacks belonging to the old brick works at Pentwyn and the long-standing houses in the centre, Club Row Snatchwood. Club Row was to suffer much grief following the Llanerch Colliery disaster of 1890, when almost every household lost a loved one, young and old.

4. Broad Street, the centre of Abersychan township in about 1908. On the left may be seen the Police Station and a little further along, a horsedrawn 'brake' is parked outside the Union Hotel waiting to transport passengers to Pontypool. Behind the gas standard is Old Road leading on to Gas Square; Old Road during this period was renowned for its slaughterhouse and all its unpleasantries so close to the public highway. A report by the County Medical Officer in 1909 suggested urgent remedial action, describing his findings as 'dark, filthy and unventilated'.

5. The years have now moved on to the early 1930s in Broad Street with a few reminders of some previous business premises that once stood here. On the left is the former shelter for the benefit of brake passengers and now converted into a small shop selling newspapers amongst other things. At the junction with Union Street is the appropriately named and since-demolished Union Hotel and the large building further along with the canopies, once housed the drapery department of Abersychan Co-operative Society; a small supermarket now occupies this site. The two cottages in the front right of the picture were demolished some years ago.

6. One unmistakable building that once graced the centre of Broad Street was the County Police Station. The building seen here with its barred windows, was built in 1885 replacing a smaller such station at the bottom of, and aptly named, Lock-up Lane. The original Trevethin Parish Lock-up, catering for local lawbreakers was built in 1837 on a piece of land provided by the British Iron Company. In this particular photograph, members of the local constabulary, which at the time consisted of a sergeant and six constables, are pictured wearing somewhat unconventional headgear for their chosen occupation, namely bush hats! These were introduced by Chief Constable Bosanquet, the idea being adopted from troops returning from the Boer War in South Africa and thought to be of some use to the peace-keepers of Great Britain. The hats of course proved to be far less suited to the weathers of Abersychan compared with the South African sun, to say nothing of the lack of protection from a possible blow from a disgruntled transgressor. After the station was de-manned, the building was temporarily used as a doctors' surgery before the modern premises were opened in Old Road in 1985. The old lock-up still stands to this day, although at present it remains unoccupied.

7./8. Two views looking up Union Street from differing periods. The upper photograph is from 1905 and displays an early picture of the Union Hotel, when William Gillman was the landlord and, close by is one of Abersychan's earliest banks. Below, the scene is just over a decade later and an elementary motor car has arrived. Most of this street has now been removed, yet at the time of this view, it housed a collection of local businesses such as Thomas Benjamin George the butcher, William Price a beer retailer and J.H. Pring the greengrocer. Those readers of a more mature standing, may also remember in later years, the fearful dental surgery at Number 38 belonging to the highly respected and master of the profession, David (Dai) Robinson!

9. An almost deserted Station Street in about 1920 and a period when there were three licensed premises on the right-hand side of the street alone. There is The Buck (still there today), The Colliers Arms (landlord Stephen Bennett) and The Railway Hotel (landlord James Coles) which was conveniently situated close to the station. Amongst these hostelries can also be seen the barbers' pole situated at Number 4, this was the hairdressing business of Mr. Alf Evans.

10. From the early 1900s this view is from Station Street looking towards the beginning of Broad Street with the popular grocers, The India and China Tea Company situated on the corner at Number 1. Immediately on the right of the picture and at the bottom of Old Lane, is the shop belonging to J. Harvey and Sons, describing themselves as Jobmasters'. On the wall opposite there is a fine display of early enamelled advertising plates which were once a most common sight, yet these days are much sought after collectors' items.

11. Another look at Station Street and the years have moved on to the most trying times for the valley, the 1930s, with almost a decade of economic hardship for everyone. On the opposite side of the road to the onlookers, is William Oliver's ladies and gents tailoring shop which was also adjacent to one of Abersychan's Post Offices for many years; the postmaster during the period of this picture was Mr. William Amson.

12. Known as The Cross, this area was the 'hub' of Abersychan in Edwardian times, forming the junction of High Street, Broad Street, Old Road and Station Street. The horse and cart on the left, belonging to Westlake's Brewery, stand outside the White Hart Hotel alongside the site of the old market. Further ahead can be seen a gas lamp in the centre of the road, which was used as the turning point for the horse-drawn public transport then operating between Abersychan and Pontypool.

13. The period has now advanced to the 1950s with some modern additions to the scenery at Station Street such as a motor car, telegraph wires and TV aerials. There is also one less public house, The Colliers Arms, which by now had been converted into a private dwelling and shop, and at about the time of this photograph, was home to Mr. Paul Murphy, later to become the the constituency M.P. and Secretary of State for Wales.

14. To have taken this view of Station Street during the 1930s, the photographer would have stood on the footbridge belonging to the GWR Station. The main building and booking office are on the bottom left with Station House next door. In the distance it will be noted that the former India and China Tea Company shop has now changed hands and belongs to the Welsh Wool and Hosiery Company.

15. Moving a short distance along Ffrwd Road and the scenery highlights the enormous changes that have affected this part of the town since being originally photographed in about 1906. After closure in 1962, the station buildings were eventually demolished in 1967. The lengthy stone-built wall seen here was also removed, making way for the present-day roadway, built in 1971-1972 and following the path of the old railway line as far as Cwmffrwd.

16. The 'general view' here illustrates the district as it appeared at the beginning of the twentieth century with many landmarks having since disappeared. In the left foreground is Gas Square, so named after the nearby Gas Works and in the distance will be seen further reminders of an industrial past, 'Pentwyn Tips'; these tips expanded considerably over the years with cinder waste from the British Ironworks. Visible in the centre of the picture is High Street, a street that gradually developed into the main shopping area as Abersychan's economy grew.

17. Pictured from the water's edge of the Afon Llwyd is the road bridge adjacent to Gas Square, and behind the bridge may be seen the smoke stack belonging to the gas works. A privately owned gas works was first built in Abersychan in 1857 before being sold off in 1869. By this time demand for coal-produced gas was increasing rapidly particularly with the introduction of street lighting. Consequently a new and larger works was built by the newly-formed Abersychan Gas Company which came into operation in January 1871. These works were to be a prominent landmark for more than a century until the introduction of North Sea Gas.

18. Overlooking the town during the 1940s, and readers may be reminded of a few landmarks, some of which are no longer standing. In the foreground for example are River Row and the whitewashed cottages of Valentine Row, sturdy nineteenth-century housing, since demolished. Behind the railway station can be seen the private residence 'Sunnybank', which has been home to a variety of local personalities over the years including colliery owners, a Member of Parliament and Justices of the Peace.

19. Another scene from the 1940s, this time showing the lower end of High Street and part of Union Street with some more ancient buildings to recall. In the foreground, just left of centre is the former Lion Hotel which these days has been converted into flats. Alongside the hotel is the building that housed the old Reform Brewery, the premises dating back to the 1832 Reform Act from which it acquired its name. In 1933 the New Reform Brewery was registered here, suggesting it to be a revitalised undertaking; this however only lasted until 1939 when the operation was finally taken over by the much larger brewer, Buchan's of Rhymney.

20. The years have marched on yet again, and the scene is now set in the 1950s. This picture is ideal for locals to reflect upon and consider just how much of Abersychan has vanished these past thirty years or so. A typical example is Union Street and just above it, in the centre of the photograph, may be seen Abersychan's own telephone exchange in High Street; this building now having been converted into business premises.

21. The centre of High Street in the early 1900s by which time it had developed into the main shopping area. With more than sixty businesses flourishing here, out-of-town shopping was hardly a consideration. The large building on the right belonged to the Abersychan, British and Talywain Industrial Co-operative Society, at the time under the capable management of Mr. John Maggs. The other substantial building opposite and standing at the junction with Bell Lane was the Bell Hotel with Edward Chapman as its landlord.

22. The cameraman is now positioned a little further down High Street, the photograph having been taken from above Brynteg. The houses on the near left still stand today as do the buildings opposite, nearside of the lamp-post. Just to the right of the post, is the Post Office and during this period, which is about 1906, it was run by Mrs. Elizabeth Brain. The shop with the large wicker basket outside was the grocery business belonging to Mr. and Mrs. Arthur Tratt.

23. Looking towards the lower end of High Street, from the top of Bell Lane in about 1915 when virtually every other building was a business of some description. The corner shop at the time belonged to Mr. Llewellyn Ingles, a reputable boot and shoe maker; he later adding the sale of bicycles to his long-established trade. All of the buildings seen on the right of this picture have since been razed to the ground.

24. This elaborate stone-built building was once the Abersychan District Workingmen's Institute. It was opened in February 1905 with Mr. William John Griffiths as its first secretary and in its heyday, the facilities included rooms for reading, recreation, billiards and even bathing. Almost a century old and minus its ornate balcony, the building still stands and now houses the local library.

25. Described as a 'Bird's Eye View', this 1907 postcard allows a more distant look at the rear of the Institute, next to the more recently demolished English Congregational Church at the top right. In the foreground and below the 'up' platform of the station with its 'Low Level' sign are some of Abersychan's older dwellings, the three-storey houses in Valentine Road.

26. Abersychan is seen as a well developed area in this picture from about 1910 and one particular old building to note, in its own grounds, is Glansychan House positioned to the right of centre of the photograph. Believed to have been built in the 1830s, it was occupied by a number of prominent citizens during its lifetime, such as Justice of the Peace William Phillips when this picture was taken. Ultimately the property was acquired by the local council in 1937 and subsequently demolished. In 1939 the grounds were declared open to the public and named as a King George's Field after the then current monarch; these days the area is better known as Glansychan Park.

27. This is Factory Lane which was originally situated between the Co-operative Stores and the Witchell boot works in High Street, and extended onwards as far as Old Lane. The lane was initially named after William Witchell's Boot Factory but, by the 1960s, long after closure of the works, it was re-named Glansychan Lane. The main property seen on this early picture, is Glansychan Cottage, which was occupied for a number of years by the chauffeur employed by the residents of Glansychan House.

28. The pictorial tour of High Street continues with this view from about 1905, looking towards the upper part of the street, an area that has altered considerably over the years. A customary delivery cart stands quietly outside the grocery and drapery store belonging to Mr. William Lewis and, although presently unoccupied, it is one of the few remaining buildings still standing in this part of High Street.

29. A truly magnificent view looking downwards from the upper end of High Street in Edwardian times. The local milkman is seen on his rounds, for these were days when milk was delivered direct from the farm in churns, the customers bringing their jugs onto the streets. All of the housing on the left has now gone, and the only building remaining from the former Co-op Stores to the top of the street, is the old Baptist Chapel. On the right hand side can be seen the Castle Inn, one of the few businesses still trading some ninety years after this photograph was taken.

30. Local residents will recognise the former houses of Club Row which were situated in Lewis Street, just below Manor Road. Seen here during the 1970s, they were superb examples of early industrial housing having been completed in about 1840. They were constructed by a local group of citizens who, in 1838, had formed an organisation to be known as the Pentwyn Benefit Building Society, intent on providing much needed and affordable housing for workers in the area. Some thirty houses were built to a high standard for the period, each of double fronted design and containing four rooms and, as will be remembered, they lasted for more than 130 years.

31. Further examples of early nineteenth-century housing are pictured here at Foundry Road, so-named after the important iron foundry that once stood between these houses and the Big Arch. The cottages were built around 1825, in typical 'two up and two down' fashion by the Hunt brothers of Pentwyn furnaces, and stood for almost 150 years before final demolition in 1972.

32. A little further up from the heart of Abersychan lies Manor Road, as pictured here in about 1918. Manor Road was built on the route of an old tramroad which was used for transporting minerals by horse-drawn trams from the local works. The original tramroad wound its way as far as Cwmffrwd, where it connected with a similar tramway from Blaenavon. The horse-drawn route then continued as far as Pontnewynydd, where the cargo would be loaded onto barges to be further shipped along the Monmouthshire Canal.

33. Exceptionally quiet times are witnessed in this scene at Old Lane almost a hundred years ago. The lane which connects Manor Road with the lower end of Abersychan has seen many changes since this Edwardian view - the exception being the nearest building here - 'Field Cottage' which still stands well.

34. This is a photograph taken from Pentwyn tips in about 1918 and is worth careful study to recall a few former landmarks. At the top left of the picture is Old Lion Terrace, where the Abersychan, British and Talywain Co-operative Society was formed in 1889. Their very first store was opened here, as was, a much less admired Company Shop owned by the British Ironworks. Just below the terrace is the Parish Church Hall which opened in 1913 and saw several uses before eventually being destroyed by fire. Some other now-disappeared sights are on the top right, Siloh Chapel which was built in 1837 and Fifteen Houses.

35. Taken from Lasgarn Woods, this view of some eighty years ago overlooks Ffrwd Road and shows the lone building of Twyn-y-Ffrwd Farm, which is to be seen above the road, left of centre. It was, from an ancient farm called 'Abersychan', that the village adopted its name. Long before any industrial establishment reached the area, the district was mere wasteland of the manor of Wentsland and Bryngwyn with 'Abersychan' being the predominant farm amongst a few smaller settlements.

36. Victoria Village which has been photographed from Talywain shows Bluett's Lane leading onto Victoria Road to the centre of the picture. The name Victoria would presumably, have been adopted from the country's longest serving monarch whilst the name Bluett, would have had a more local flavour in that Rev. Bluett was the first vicar of the parish and thus merited a certain recognition.

37. All is extremely quiet on Ffrwd Road during the early years of this century. At the junction with Lower Harpers Road is the Victoria Council School which had opened in 1903, shortly before this picture was taken. Close by can be seen the cottages of School Lane which have now been replaced by modern housing and, on this photograph, it can be seen that the land at the side of the road was once used as a refuse tip.

38. Another scene at Ffrwd Road from the same period as the previous photograph, and on this occasion looking towards the Twyn-y-Ffrwd Inn, to the right, with Lasgarn Woods in the background. On the left of the picture is the house known as 'Rose Cottage' which, as to be expected, has seen many improvements since. This particular residence is believed to have been built around the year 1850.

39. Vicarage Terrace Cwmffrwd as the houses appeared a short while after construction in 1911. Just out of sight and set in grounds on the right is the parish vicarage, hence the name given to this row of dwellings. The photographer at the time, Mr. Ernest Bush of Cardiff, would have been positioned just above the old railway halt at Cwmffrwd which is now the site of a motor vehicle service station.

40. An idyllic scene at Cwmffrwd in 1912 with Waterworks Lane and the ancient bridge spanning the Afon Llwyd. The cottages on the far left have since benefited from extensive modernisation and conversion into a single dwelling. On the right is Lasgarn Cottage which was once part of the Hanbury Estate and occupied by the woodcutter. Approximately 160 years old, the original house has seen necessary improvements and an extension during its long history but is still known locally as the Woodman's Cottage.

41. The date of this photograph is confirmed as April 29th 1962, the last day a passenger train travelled through Cwmffrwd's level crossing, which is seen being crossed by local farmer Mr. Bill Davies. Mr. Davies farmed at Nant-y-Mailor which is situated above the reservoir near the quarries bearing the same name.

42. A panoramic view that provides some further evidence of Abersychan's industrial past. In the centre may be seen the path of a tramway incline which was constructed from Talywain to Twyn-y-Ffrwd by the Ebbw Vale Company, who in 1852 had acquired the business of the British Ironworks. Minerals were carried in trams which were operated by a stationary steam engine system to the valley below, then re-loaded onto wagons running on the new Pontypool to Blaenavon railway line which had opened in 1854. This however was a slow and costly method of moving materials, which was only alleviated when the branch line from Trevethin Junction to Talywain was opened in 1879.

43. Abersychan district as it looked from an aircraft during the 1920s with Pentwyn nearest to the camera. Some immediate features to note include the brickworks, owned by the Abersychan Brick Company and further to the right is Pentwyn railway halt, which was opened in 1912 by the Great Western Railway. The line itself was constructed more than thirty years earlier; to join with the branch line from Brynmawr at Talywain; just beyond Pentwyn Halt a short branch headed off and passed through the Big Arch to reach the British Ironworks.

44. A view of the village of Pentwyn, the age of which can be judged by the absence of the Mission Hall which was constructed in 1913. On the right is Pentwyn Terrace with Numbers 5 and 7 being utilised as shops and in the background are Lethbridge Terrace on the left with the end house of Severn View on the right. Today's residents of Lethbridge Terrace may be interested to know that their properties were available ninety years ago at a rent of 27$\frac{1}{2}$p per week, whilst those in Severn View were let at 37$\frac{1}{2}$p (all rents to include the supply of water).

45. At first glance this final picture in the opening chapter may be a little difficult to place. It is however, the main road looking north towards Blaenavon, and the prominent building in the centre is the Rising Sun Inn at Cwmffrwd. It can be seen that the road has not yet been constructed adjacent to the inn but diverges to the left, up Vicarage Lane and beyond. The rough-looking track on the right of the photograph is the entrance to Waterworks Lane.

CHAPTER 2

Talywain, Garndiffaith and Varteg

46. Viaduct Road is the location of this early Victorian cottage which was similar in design to a number of others scattered about the area. Now demolished, it once stood almost beneath the Garndiffaith and Talywain viaduct, an arch of which can be seen in the background. Unfortunately it has not been possible to trace the identity of the family seen here but, the period is about 1910.

47./48. Two scenes of Pisgah Road from years gone by. On the upper photograph is Pisgah Chapel as it appeared before the major alterations of 1930, the larger building attached being the Sunday Schoolroom which was opened in 1909. In the lower picture, a horse and cart struggle up Pisgah Hill and in the background is the newly constructed Garndiffaith Junction signal box.

49. The former British Schools which were a feature of Church Road for more than 130 years and now, just one more memory for the residents of Talywain. Church Road itself stretches from the top of High Street Abersychan almost to the Parish Church at Talywain, and the school built here, once catered for the largest number of pupils in the Abersychan district.

50. An early view of part of Commercial Road Talywain as it appeared in about 1905, before any shops or housing were constructed on the nearside of the road. The cottages furthest to the right, behind the corner shop are situated on Bluett's Road, whilst moving along Commercial Road to the second telegraph pole, just left of centre, are the buildings which were demolished a few years later. This demolition was to make way for the building of Talywain's branch of the Co-op.

51. Albert Road some eighty years ago when there was little need for a respectable road surface prior to any motorised transport. The level-crossing gates at the end of the road are closed, suggesting perhaps that railway traffic had priority here at the time. This road was once home to five public houses, two of which are seen on this photograph. On the immediate left is the Railway Inn with Mr. John Lloyd as the proprietor and further along is the Albert Inn. With the exception of three remaining cottages, the row as far as the Albert Inn has now been removed.

52. Emlyn Terrace which during the period of this picture was amidst the industrial area of Talywain. On the opposite side of the road, on land now partly occupied by the rugby ground, stood the Scarlet Ferric Oxide Company or perhaps better known as the chemical works. When this closed in the early 1900s, the site was taken over by the John Paton ballast crushing plant. The photograph, was taken from a spot near 'Thickpenny's Corner', so named after tradesman Edward Thickpenny whose shop was nearby. This shop was originally yet another Talywain public house, the Black Horse.

53. A much-changed scene at Garndiffaith as viewed from the viaduct, with the exceptionally steep, lower end of High Street in the centre. On the extreme upper left is the former Cinder Row which overlooked the infamous ash tip. Directly below the tip some gentlemen are seen walking along an area which, for some undefined reason, is still known as 'The Rookery'. On the far right is the Wesleyan Chapel which was situated in Earl Street.

54. Commercial Road facing in the direction of the railway crossing, the lines of which are receiving some maintenance work. The building on the right with the porch, is Talywain's Post and Telegraph Office which was managed by Miss Annie Barnfield when this photograph was taken. The old Post Office is now gone but the larger building further along the road is still in business, the Globe Inn.

55. Here is a another view of Commercial Road although this time, the years have moved on to the late 1920s. The approaching bus, bound for Abersychan, belongs to the Eastern Valley Motor Services whose garages were at Garndiffaith and Pontnewynydd. Just to the left of the bus is another old Talywain landmark, Golynos Junction signal box and the ladies in the picture stand outside the Golynos Hotel, then managed by Mr.Tom Carter.

56. A 1960s expansive view of Talywain overlooking Farm Road in the centre. A Western Welsh bus is seen passing by 'The Castle' which is a 'listed building', the cottage dating back to the 16th or 17th century. To the left of The Castle is the area known as Castle Wood and on the far right are Castle Pond railway sidings. Talywain was quite an important railway junction at one time, it being linked to most of the surrounding collieries in the Eastern Valley and used as the marshalling area for coal wagons. The sidings were finally closed in November 1971.

57./58. Two views looking in opposite directions which were taken from the old railway bridge on Harpers Road. Above is a pre-1920 scene showing a once-popular meeting place for the locals, the Six Bells Inn; the property has since been converted into flats. In the lower picture and just behind the lamp-post, is the age-old Green Meadow Farm which was still a working farm until about 1970. Although presently derelict, plans have recently been approved to convert the premises into living accommodation which will externally represent this 1930s appearance.

59. A 'bird's eye view' of Garndiffaith as it appeared during the 1930s. Many of the houses and cottages have long been demolished, some having been replaced by more modern buildings. To assist today's readers in locating the scene, in the right foreground is the top end of Harpers Road with St. John's Church on Stanley Road in the centre of the picture.

60. Another aerial picture from the 1930s provides an exquisite view of the Garndiffaith and Talywain viaduct. Having survived for more than 120 years, the structure is another fine example of Victorian railway workmanship, it being constructed in the years 1876-77 by engineer John Gardner. The viaduct was originally built for the London and North Western Railway Company whose branch line from Brynmawr to Blaenavon, was further extended as far as Talywain station.

61. A nostalgic look at what was once the upper part of High Street. The first premises at the corner with Percy Street is the Post Office and Stationers, which was ably managed by Miss Lillian Lockyer and next door, was one of Garndiffaith's many hostelries, The Mason's Arms. The larger building further up the street was, in later years, the shop belonging to Mr. W. Herbert, subsequently to be purchased by the local Co-operative Society.

62. A more recent scene at Garndiffaith, yet even since this photograph was taken in the 1970s, all that remains today is the Hanbury Hotel. Next to the hotel was the Co-op butcher's shop which was originally yet another licensed hostelry, the White Lion. Adjoining the butchery was the gent's outfitting department, this in earlier times being a confectionery and boot shop owned by the Templar family. The demolition workers eventually arrived in this part of the village in 1981.

42

63. A traditional centre of community activities in the Welsh valleys was once the local workmen's institute, often financed entirely by the workers themselves. Garndiffaith was fortunate in receiving some additional funding from the benevolent Scotsman Andrew Carnegie, who did much to promote well-being in south Wales. The foundation stone of Garndiffaith Institute was laid in 1908 and eventually, costing some £1800, boasted a public hall with seating for 600 and the addition of a free library, reading room and popular billiard room. Over the years the Institute was managed and maintained by voluntary contributions of two pence per week from miners of the district, successfully enough for the main hall to be converted into a cinema with the arrival of movie films. Changing times however saw decline, closure and dereliction of the building for a number of years until revitalised interest during the 1980s, when it was completely renovated and re-opened in 1987. Unfortunately the billiards room, library and reading room did not survive but to locals however, the building that still stands will probably be forever known as 'The Garn Hall'.

64. A typical view towards the lower end of High Street in about 1922, the gradient here presenting numerous problems for some Garndiffaith residents. Heavy rains were a nightmare, with water cascading down the street, often finding its way straight into peoples' homes. The horse and cart are stood at the entrance to Chapel Lane with a further selection of the many local 'Pubs' to be seen such as the Butcher's Arms, the large building at the top right and the Little Crown, the second building from the top left.

65. The viaduct as seen in the year 1908, with a goods train loaded with pit-props heading towards Blaenavon. A short distance past the viaduct stood Six Bells Halt which was built later, in 1912, by the G.W.R. to serve local railway passengers; the halt in subsequent years changed its name to Garndiffaith Halt. Now utilised as a cycle track and walkway, the viaduct still stands firm, with the hearts of the local Pontypool and Blaenavon Railway Society members hoping one day to extend their services as far as this potential railway monument.

66. Just one motor car and a few pedestrians are present in Stanley Road during the late 1930s. This road acquired its name from Dr. Stanley Verity who had followed in the footsteps of his father, Dr. Abraham Robert Verity, to become a popular local practitioner. The elder Dr. Verity, had arrived in Garndiffaith in the nineteenth century, to continue with the early medical establishment of a Dr. Davies.

67. The lower end of Herberts Road with the lady on the left of the picture standing in the lane leading to Davies Court. Of the three gentlemen stood on the right, at the entrance to the Institute, two have been identified as Mr. Dick Webb and Mr. Mann. The shop with the canopy may be remembered by some as being a Temperance Bar in later years, adjacent to the Fish and Chip Shop. Further along the road and opposite the old Police Station, a horse and trap carries one of Garndiffaith's doctors on his 'rounds' some eighty years ago.

68. This is Co-operative Terrace which is situated at the top end of Herberts Road, a row of houses that has stood the test of time. A piece of land was purchased here in the early 1900s by Mr. Abel Myers, Abersychan's pawnbroker, who built the first nine houses, the remainder being constructed by two other gentlemen. Some time after completion, the local Co-operative Society purchased the properties from Mr. Myers for the princely sum of £110 each! At the far end of the terrace is the road junction known as Coombes' Cross, so named after a former local police officer, Constable Coombes who once resided at a nearby cottage, since demolished.

69. A surviving photograph of the Balance Houses at Garndiffaith which were appropriately named after the neighbouring Balance Pits. The pond seen in the foreground was for feeding the water-operating system used at the pits, and is described in more detail in the industrial chapter of this book.

70. This was once a very familiar scene, the former bus terminus at Garndiffaith. The building has seen a number of uses and one that may be remembered, was the garage and car business opened in 1954 by Glyn and Jean Davies. Some other prominent buildings include the Workmen's Club (top centre) and the now-demolished houses adjacent to Butlers Lane. Another reminder of bygone days is the sight of a few colliers heading home, probably from a shift's work at Lower Varteg Colliery.

71. Moving further up the valley to Varteg Lane, and the scene is from around the year 1920. On close examination of this photograph it will be noted that the area is still under development, with the house furthest away on the left awaiting completion by the builders. Just visible below, and to the left of the telegraph pole, is a shop which in later years was to become the confectionery store belonging to Miss Alice Bees.

72. A view of what was probably the oldest and earliest occupied part of the original hamlet of Varteg. The houses in the centre were strongly associated with Varteg's nineteenth-century industrial undertakings, particularly the larger three-storey building which once housed the dreaded 'Company Shop', with its outrageous prices and methods of trading. In the background is Gladstone Terrace, houses that were built in the 1890s on the site of a tramroad used by the old ironworks; these works were once situated a short distance to the right of the photograph.

73./74. Two photographs that illustrate some more historical buildings at Varteg, namely the old Wesleyan Chapel and Institute. The chapel seen here in 1908, was founded in about 1823 and in later years was also utilised as a schoolroom. A much needed larger Workmen's Institute was erected on the same site in 1919, this proving to be a most popular meeting place consisting of a library, reading rooms and a billiards hall housing three full-sized tables. The Institute is pictured in the lower photograph in about 1920 and was to remain the centre of social activity in the village for many years until eventual demolition in 1985. To the right of the new Institute may be seen the 'later' Wesleyan Chapel, which was built during the years 1868-69.

75. This photograph may remind some senior readers of the winter blizzards of 1947 and the ensuing chaos. Industry, transport and communications came to a standstill, with snowdrifts that reached bedroom windows being a most common sight. Virtually cut off from the outside world, there were soon major concerns regarding food supplies to the village of Varteg and some volunteer emergency digging is witnessed here. The men are seen attempting a route towards Garndiffaith and they include Albert Jones and Ernest Roden (1st and 2nd left) with Cliff Weeks on the right; unfortunately it has not been possible to trace the names of the two gentlemen in the centre.

76. This group of houses was known as Spring Gardens, once situated between the Band Hall and Coke Yard, the Coke Yard being developed into a ground for Varteg's cricket players. Amongst Spring Gardens' residents was one Gunner Abraham Evans, a local hero who had fought in one of the British Army's most famous battles, that at Rorke's Drift South Africa in 1879. Despite being hospitalised from wounds received, Gunner Evans gave valuable assistance in removing his fellow comrades to safety whilst the building was under attack. He continued his military career, participating in numerous other skirmishes after the Zulu campaign and was later honoured with an introduction to Queen Victoria.

77. Varteg's one-time main street with the twenty houses belonging to Slate Row on the left, and the Primitive Methodist chapel at the bottom. The opposite side of the street was for some reason originally called 'Teetotal Row', subsequently to be officially re-named as Post Office Row. This name was adopted in later years, following the opening of Varteg's first Post Office in the 1850s at Number 56, it being situated approximately where the lady furthest from the camera stands. When this picture was taken in 1906, Mr. Edward Webster was Sub-Postmaster, he also applying his skills as a local renowned boot manufacturer.

78. Kear's Row in the 1950s and the building that was at one time the Garndiffaith and Varteg Co-op, has now been converted into two private houses. The occupiers were the Thomas and Morris families and Mr. Thomas's Coal Board delivery lorry is parked alongside. A map of 1882 also suggests that the site at one time, housed licensed premises belonging to the Varteg Brewery Co.

79. Varteg can lay claim to be the oldest village community in the Urban District of Abersychan, it developing from the earliest years of the nineteenth century. Numerous rows of houses began to appear to accommodate a growing population which, at its peak, was to approach 1500. Amongst those houses were Incline Row, Post Office Row, Slate Row and The Square and of course a number of necessary shops. This picture is from Edwardian times and shows Slate Row on the far left. Cross Row in the centre and Kear's Row on the far left.

53

80. Salisbury Terrace with its unique slate-covered frontage was constructed during the last decade of the nineteenth century and is pictured here in about 1918. The first house at the lower end, much larger in design and with an added 'front garden', was originally occupied by a senior member of the local collieries. A few doors up at Number 3, a notice board is on display, and this is where the local 'Bobby' once resided.

81. 'Ten Houses' - otherwise known as Chapel Terrace, due to its close proximity to the Wesleyan chapel. On the opposite side of the road was the Memorial Hall, which was built in 1922 in memory of those who lost their lives in the Great War of 1914-1918. The local Silver Band made particular use of the building for many years, it always being referred to as 'The Band Hall' by the local community. Ultimately suffering from severe fire damage and with an estimate of repairs amounting to £30,000 the owners, British Coal, were persuaded to sell the building to the area's community association for the nominal sum of just one pound! The understanding being that it would be converted for community use. Unfortunately, this did not materialise and subsequently the hall was razed to the ground.

82./83. Summerhill Varteg, where more true examples of workers' housing were to be found. Built in the early 1800s in a 'back-to-back format' and named 'Twenty Houses', they were later re-named Summerhill North and Summerhill South but, to locals however, were to be referred to as 'Camelback' or 'Humpback Row' due to their unusual shape. The name Twenty Houses also raises a question, as the row actually consisted of twenty-four dwellings. Both of these pictures date from about 1908, the upper photograph of Summerhill North providing an interesting view of the stable-styled doors which were an integral part in the design of this type of housing. These properties were lived-in for almost 150 years before final demolition.

84. A distant view of 'The Snailcreep', the long and winding course connecting Varteg with Cwmavon, a route often confused with nearby Shop Road which also joins the two villages. This picture additionally shows two former, and relatively close railway stations; Varteg in the top right, which stood on the London and North Western line with Blaenavon High Level as its next stop up the valley and, in the foreground, Cwmavon Halt on the Great Western line, with Blaenavon Low Level as its terminus.

85. Cwmavon's new road bridges which were opened to traffic in 1932, are seen here in about 1935 with a veteran Leyland bus on its way to Pontypool. In the background is Forge Row, one of the last surviving and best preserved examples of nineteenth-century housing in the area. Built in 1805 as dwellings for employees of nearby Varteg Forge, they are now 'listed' buildings and have been fully restored and under private ownership.

CHAPTER 3

Places of Worship and Learning

86. The church of St.Thomas and Parish Church of Abersychan, situated in the heart of Talywain is pictured here in about 1920. Prior to the building of St.Thomas's, conformist worship in the district was held in some unusual venues such as the Club Room belonging to the Old Lion Hotel. As time advanced through the beginning of the nineteenth century, worshippers gradually progressed to a building of their own, a corrugated iron structure which was erected on the site of the church seen above. Naturally as the population and congregations of the area steadily increased, by the year 1830 it was decided that a new and more prestigious church building should be considered. Mostly financed by the British Iron Company, work commenced on St. Thomas's in April 1831, the task undertaken by contractor Mr. John Lane of Pontypool. This new church, built in the early English style, was finally completed in the Autumn of 1832 and the first Divine Service was held there on the morning of September 10th. With space for 480 sittings, the church was packed to capacity with Rev. Jones of Trevethin leading the service and Rev. Rees of Blaina preaching the sermon. As English was not the widespread and understood language of many local people at the time, an additional service was held in the afternoon, this time in the more familiar Welsh tongue. The arrangement thereafter, and one that lasted for many years was, that English and Welsh Services would be conducted on alternate Sundays. For the first twelve years of St. Thomas's, worship was led by numerous religious dignitaries until 1844, when it was constituted into an Ecclesiastical Parish and the first Parish Vicar was appointed. He was Rev. F.R. Bluett of Devon who was temporarily accommodated at Bailey Glas Farm whilst the vicarage was being built, he serving as a most respected leader in the community until his death in 1871. Regrettably, and following present trends, the church has been deprived of much of its following and the building stands derelict, the remaining congregation now meeting in a hall close by.

87. The Rev. F.R.P.C. Bluett B.A. (1800-1871) first Vicar of St. Thomas's who served from 1844 to 1871.

88. A group photograph which was taken at Abersychan Congregational Church in about 1945. Judging by the trophy shields proudly displayed, the church members and children have some significant achievement to celebrate. The Minister at the time was Reverend Glyndwr Harris, who is stood on the far left of the group. Also identified is Mrs. Ann Hodder who is seen second from the left, in the third row from the front, Mrs. Hodder having kindly loaned the original photograph.

89. The Congregational Church at Abersychan as it looked in its prime, some ninety years ago. The church building itself was demolished in 1998 but the church hall, seen behind, has survived and is presently used as a community hall. The original manse to the right of the church unfortunately suffered bomb damage during World War Two and was later pulled down altogether; a replacement dwelling was built after the war and although now privately owned, is still called 'The Manse'.

90. Noddfa Baptist Chapel which still stands proudly in Church Road Abersychan was founded in 1846, to become the second Baptist chapel in the town. Noddfa, during that period of time, was probably a saviour to many local followers of the Baptist faith as it was purposely established for the Welsh-only speaking members of the community.

91. The stage is set beneath the mighty organ pipes of Noddfa Baptist for an annual Sunday School Anniversary, and the year is thought to be about 1957. Former pupils of local Sunday Schools may also remember a traditional treat once the Anniversary had been celebrated, the proverbial outing to the seaside! Rev. N. Priday is surrounded by fifty-eight members of his flock in this picture though unfortunately, it has not been possible to identify many of their names. However, amongst the gathering are to be seen Christine Butcher, Susan Howells, Barry Powell, Diane Butcher, Jennifer McComb, several members of the Bustin family and Tina, Jennifer and Jeremy Mayers.

92. An exceptionally early photograph of Pisgah Baptist Chapel in about 1902. Pisgah was opened for worship in the year 1828 and is a perfect example of the devotion to the faith in earlier years. It is recorded that much of the stone used in the original construction was retrieved from the Afon Ffrwd and carried up the hill by female helpers. A Sunday School building was added to the chapel in 1909 with further improvements and alterations in the early 1930s.

93. The first Catholic church in Abersychan was built at Manor Road in the year 1863. Constructed of corrugated iron and timber it was later damaged by fire and consequently demolished. This picture however, is of the contemporary-designed replacement church which was built at a new location in Church Road Talywain, and dedicated to St.Francis of Assisi.

94. St. John's Parish Church in Stanley Road Garndiffaith which was built in 1932. Permission was first granted to build a church at Garndiffaith as early as 1896, the project foundering however when it was realised that the plans were encroaching on part of the burial ground. Following a number of years of temporary accommodation in such unlikely places as the Hanbury Hotel and Workmen's Hall, a more permanent building was eventually erected in 1913 which is seen on the rear right of the photograph. This served its purpose until 1932 when the present structure, in fine Gothic style was completed. The old 1913 building was demolished in 1980.

95. Members of Snatchwood Methodist Sunday School (formerly the Primitive Methodist Abersychan), display their award after winning the Sunday Schools' Scripture Examination Challenge Shield in about 1934. The proud teachers are Mr. Herbert Dean on the left and Mr. Llewellyn Jones on the right. A few pupils' names can be recalled and the boys include Billy Smith, Ivor and Wilf Barrett and Berwyn Smith. The ladies left to right are ?, Florence Jones, Miss Milsom, Muriel Hawkins, Miss Parker and Gladys Llewellyn.

96. Yet another ancient place of worship was Sardis Congregationalist Chapel which may be remembered at the rear of High Street and Percy Street in Garndiffaith. Now demolished, Sardis was opened in about 1830, a time when nonconformist chapels were rapidly gathering in popularity in opposition to the Established Church.

97. The Calvinistic following was founded by the French theologian Jean (John) Calvin during the 16th Century, it taking a number of years before becoming acceptable in Great Britain. Above is a photograph of the Calvinistic Methodist Presbyterian Tabernacle Chapel which was built at Garndiffaith in 1828. Rebuilt in 1883, it stood in Chapel Lane for 150 years before closure and final demolition in 1978.

98. The founder of Methodism in this country was the distinguished English preacher John Wesley, who lived from 1703-1791. Wesley led rousing and inspiring tours of the Welsh valleys during the eighteenth century, preaching the Gospel and establishing the long-standing following. The Wesleyan Chapel in Earl Street was Garndiffaith's largest such venue for nonconformist worship.

99. Bethel Primitive Methodist Chapel in Herberts Road was originally built in the year 1849. Pictured here in about 1908, Bethel is one of the few to have survived these changing times and 150th Anniversary celebrations were held here in March 1999.

100. It is almost fifty years since this place of worship was part of the scenery at Varteg. Here is the Primitive Methodist Chapel which stood at the bottom of Slate Row having been erected in 1872 when chapel congregations were plentiful. As the population of Varteg gradually decreased however, so did the need for its number of chapels and so by 1952, it became necessary for the 'Prims' to amalgamate with the nearby Wesleyan Chapel. The Primitive Methodist was eventually razed to the ground in 1955.

101. The former Wesleyan Chapel at Varteg pictured in about 1904. The foundation stone of this chapel was laid on November 16th 1868 by Mrs. John Vipond, wife of the local colliery owner. The chapel was completed the following year and opened for worship on September 9th 1869. The original design contained a large circular window at the front, which can be seen as having been bricked up for some reason in this photograph. The last services were held here in January 1996, the building then being converted into a community centre. This in turn suffered severe fire damage, requiring further renovation before its re-opening in 1999.

102. A traditional Sunday School Anniversary attracts a large gathering at the Wesleyan Varteg, in about 1952. The children unfortunately are too numerous to identify on this occasion but, the adults include, on the left - Elsie Pugsley, Mrs. Crease and Margaret Crease and on the right are Ruth Jones and Godfrey Johns.

103. Another 1950s scene from the Wesleyan which includes the following. Gentlemen - Charlie Tanner, Terry Jones, Robert James, Aubrey Kinnersley, Stan Morris, Terry Bath, Harry Wyatt, Godfrey Johns and Joe Stacey. Ladies - Middle Row: Margaret Crease, Ruth Jones, Cilla Harris, Mrs. Crease, Mrs. Miller, Joan Caton and unknown. Front: Rene Harris, Elsie Pugsley, Ms. Butcher, Pauline Carey, Margaret Evans, Jean Iley, Joan Clark, Mary Williams and Barbara Wood.

104. High Street Baptist Chapel was the first nonconformist church in Abersychan, it being founded in 1827. Considering that the predominant language in the district was Welsh at the time, this chapel was firmly established to cater for the English tongue alone. Thankfully High Street Church still survives to serve the faithful Baptists of the town.

105. Another long-standing religious establishment still to be found in High Street is Trinity Methodist Church. In the capable hands of local minister Reverend Ken Morgan, services are regularly held here each Sunday morning.

106. The pupils of Victoria School 'Top Class' in 1955 accompanied by their teacher Miss Maggs who is seen on the right. From left to right the pupils are - Back Row: Michael Tripp, Terry Williams, David Parfitt, Billy Price and Terry Hale. Middle: Norman Burgess, Derek Bodenham, Alban Bult, Gerald Davies, Clifford Harrison, Pat Latham, Sandra Sewell, Ann Barnbrook, Brian Harrison, David Howells, Fred Probyn, Graham Jones and Howard Evans. Front: Valerie Owen, Christine Simons, Ruth Chivers, Sheila Moore, Sandra Garland, Susan Lindridge, Jacqueline Heard, Maureen Whittington, Frances Beard, Freda Roberts and Janice Hopkins.

107. Lower Garndiffaith Board School as it looked in the year 1905 when Mr. Thomas Brown was headmaster and Mrs. Charlotte Hankins headmistress. Built on land owned by the Marquis of Abergavenny, the school was opened on May 26th 1903. Costing a very substantial sum for the period, some £6000, it catered for 298 mixed scholars and 149 infants; the school was given its more familiar name of Abersychan Victoria Council School in 1906.

108. Some of the junior pupils with teacher Mrs. Gough at the Victoria School in 1959. Regrettably only a few names have come to light at the time of publication and they are, left to right - Back: John Clark (2nd), Anthony Edwards (5th), Derek Keenan (7th). Middle: Peter Shorthouse (5th), Stuart Harrison (9th). Front: Jean Mark (4th), Elizabeth Carey (5th).

109. An early picture of the 'British School' at Talywain, an educational landmark in the area since the nineteenth century. The name 'British' was adapted from the school's original founders, the British Iron Company who, as important employers in the district, were keen to promote education for their workers' children. Opening in 1860, the school could accommodate 800 pupils and further extensions in 1893 pushed the total to 900. By the early 1880s however, the Iron Company fell into decline and could no longer afford to maintain their liabilities and consequently the school was taken over by the Trevethin School Board. Thereafter, it saw continued service until closure in 1980 and eventual demolition during the 1990s.

110. A class photograph at the British School during the 1960s and most of the pupils can be recognised as follows - Back: Les Horler, Eddie Wilmott, Tony Luffman, ?, Gill Ralph, Kim Richards, Chris Brandon, ?, ?, and Mr. John Prince (Teacher). First Row: Phil Touhig, Master Drew, Janet Williams, Ann Harding, ?, John Bustin, Michael Britton, ?. Front: David Stephens and Noddy Harris.

111. The pupils of Form 3b at the British School pose for a photograph with their teacher in 1973. Seen left to right are - Back Row: Donald Mainwaring, Robert Dix, John Richards, Stephen Cornfield, Adrian Saunders, Dennis Reid, Michael Price and Alan Parfitt. Third Row: Mr. E. Taylor (Teacher), Karen Powell, Peggy Rawlings, Desree Woods, Janet Howells, Beverley Allaway, Linda Hobbs, Sherida Gronow and Susan Waters. Second Row: Julie Randall, Jacqueline Rosser, Dawn Stark, Tania Williams, Marilyn Touhig, Sharon Matthews and Elaine Drew. Front: John Gullis and Martin Watkins.

112. The year is uncertain but the photograph probably dates from the 1930s and shows a rugby team from St. Francis R.C. School Abersychan. Seen left to right are - Back: Derek Nutt, Dennis Whitehouse, George Jones, Charlie Turner, Glyn Sulway, Don Mahoney, William Robinson and Tom Basham. Middle: Dennis Johnson, William Beal, Mr. Tom Smith (Headmaster), John Touhig and Fred Hewison. Front: Tom Price, John Donovan and Donald Trehern.

113. The Higher Elementary School at Abersychan which was built near Manor Road in 1914, may be considered quite modern compared with the number of nineteenth-century schools that once stood in the area. This school was intended for 250 mixed pupils and also served as a pupil-teachers' centre, and at the time of this photograph in about 1923, Mr. John Clement James was the headmaster and Miss Laura Lewis the senior mistress. In later years it became the Abersychan Grammar School and is now the site of the Comprehensive.

114. The staff at Abersychan's Grammar School are pictured here in 1950 and their names will be remembered as follows, reading left to right. Back: Madamoiselle Clare, Trevor Vaughan, Trevor Edwards, Mr. L. Powell, Mr. J.O. Evans, Francis Hicks, Harry Wilcox, Arthur Jacobs, Ernest Pitt and Sheila Bartlett. Front: Mr. Melville Jones J.P., Margaret Gulwell, Miss P. Evans, Miss E. Thomas, Mr. Horace J. Padfield (Headmaster), Hedley Jacobs, Miss Lewis, Mrs. Thompson and Professor Alfred Thompson.

115. A rugby fifteen from the Abersychan Mining and Technical Institute in the 1947-48 season. In the back row are Messrs. Cooper, Langley, ?, Barnard, Critchfield, Reagan, Reardon, Green and Newbury. Seated: Mr. Ronald Smith (Science), Messrs. MacDowell, Graham Jones, Mr. Thomas Windsor (Headmaster), Critchfield, Jenkins and Mr. Robinson (Woodwork). Front: Messrs. Morgan and Samuels.

116. The middle school rugby team with some members of staff at Abersychan Grammar in 1945-46. Back Row: Brian Ashman, Cyril Sayce, Roy Flowers, Jack Bradstreet, Donald Williams, John S. Williams, John Barnes, ?, David Eastman and Alan Jenkins. Middle: Mr. Francis Hicks (Science), Gwyn Clark, Raymond Wall, Ralph Williams, Mr. Clement James (Headmaster), Tom Prosser, Donald Wilcox, David Morgan and Mr. Ernest Pitt (History). Front: Ronald Leighton, Rodney Baker, Ronald Williams, Walter Murgatroyd, John Williams and John Coates.

117. The Board Schools as they were known, were opened at Garndiffaith in May 1876 and are pictured here in 1906 when Mr. John Roxburgh and Mrs. Millard were master and mistress in charge. Originally built with scope for more than 400 pupils, further extensions took place in 1889 and by 1905 a new infants' department was added, bringing capacity up to almost 700 children. As with most schools in the district before the passing of the Education Act, Garndiffaith was fee-paying and a charge of 2d (1p) per week was levied for lessons. This school was demolished in March 1999, the teaching facilities combining with Varteg in new premises known as Garnteg.

118. Some possible future stars are pictured here after performing in a school play at Garndiffaith during the late 1940s, and a few faces may be recognised as Brian Lloyd, Anne Philpot, Jean Viner, Mike Hancock, Susan Weeks, Yolande Forsey, Christine Parry, Christine Harris, Betty Jones, Pam Gould, Jacqueline Anslow and Sylvia Price.

119. A photograph taken in the yard at Garndiffaith Junior School during the early 1960s. They are named from the left as follows - Back: Mr. Lewis, John Felton, Robert Owen, Graham Stark, David Trinder, Gwillam Williams, Les Brown, Spencer Luffman, Glyn Harris, David Powell, Raymond Powell, Mr. Davies (Headmaster). Middle: Jan Webb, Elizabeth Evans, Ella Miles, Christine Clark, unknown, Jane Skipsey, Christine Leonard, Barnadette Meacham, Carol Williams, Jill Price, David Touhig. Front: Graham Forward, Robert Thomas, Ian Samuels, Leslie Stevens, David James, Ken Williams, John Davies, J. Smith.

120. The School Band at Pentwyn in the late 1930s and the players are - Back Standing: Mauvid Williams, Joan Black, Ken Parry, David Jones, Wilf White and Ken Rosser. Middle Row Seated: Ron Williams, Marjorie Sulway, Myril Templar, Marjorie Trollope and Charlie Waite. The Drummers: Brian Hodder and Reg Cooper. Front: Margaret Crandon, Jayne Gwyn, Eddie Jones, Margaret Jones, Margaret Rees and Ken Green.

121. Hopefully there are a few readers whose faces appear on this school photograph taken at Pentwyn in 1930 and the pupils are named as follows, left to right. Back: Granville Rees, unknown, Albert Kitch, George Peacock, Jack Thomas, Sid Parry, Danny Dobbs, Bob Sweeting and unknown. Third Row: Dicky Davies, Master Whitton, Joan Thomas, R. Whitehouse, Queenie Blake, Mel Roden, Margy Parfitt, Marion Lucas and Mary Hale. Second Row: Gwyn Richards, G. Cox, Dot Wells, Ceridwen Davies, Nancy Dobbs, ?, Gwen Tudgay, Molly Blake and Ceinwen Morgan. Front: Unknown, Thelma Harris and unknown.

122. A further picture from Pentwyn School in about 1930 showing teacher Enid Coombs with some of her pupils. Back Row: Scott Samuel, Ken Cooper, Malcolm Warns and Roger Daniels. Third Row: Enid Coombs, ?, ?, Reggie Davies, Ken Roderick, Ivor Smith, Pat Stone, Sheila Hopkins and unknown. Second Row: Jean Pritchard (4th left) Front: ?, Norman Rees, Ms. Bailey.

123. Varteg Schools, the first section of which, with the bell tower, was built for infants in 1892. As the child population of Varteg was increasing quite rapidly during this period, the school was intended to ease the overcrowding at the Board School held in the old Wesleyan Chapel. The new school however, required further extensions by 1904 and now held spaces for 450 juniors and infants. The above photograph is from about 1908 when Mr. John Harvey was headmaster, assisted by Miss Edith Thomas.

124. This picture provides the opportunity to view one of the infants' classrooms at Varteg School during the 1930s and amongst the children are David Bendall, Derek Parry, Ken Cox, Terry Bath, Derek Johns, Master Gorman, Les Evans, Harry Pritchard and Billy Woods.

125. Prior to the introduction of Comprehensive schooling in the 1980s, pupils' progression from junior to grammar school education was determined by the results of the 'Eleven Plus Exam'. The above photograph was taken at Varteg Junior in 1951 and shows a number of children who had passed their exam that year. At the back are headmaster Mr. Hooper and fellow teacher Mr. Mogford. The pupils are - Middle: Sheila Jones, Gwyn Pritchard, Howard Hobbs and Iris Jones. Front: Janet Brace, Joan Price, Bryan Roden, Howard Loxton, Josie Williams and Joyce Evans.

126. The years have now moved along to about 1956 at Varteg School and some of the pupils' names have been traced as follows - Back Row: Mr. Mogford (Teacher), Jimmy Goodhall, Raymond ?, ?, Grenville Boulter, Michael Quigley, Gerald Arnott, Robert Price, Brian Roynon and Donald Weeks. Third Row: Mary Howells, Valerie Wilmott, Sandra Butcher, ?, Elaine Hobbs, Susan George, Carol Jones, ?, Dawn Price and Gillian Morgan. Second Row: Yvonne ?, Sandra Weeks, Christine Jones, Susan Butcher, Hazel Wall, Ms. Hewitt, Carol Kelham, Ruth Clements, Ann Roynon and Jennifer Jones. Front: Robert Smith, John Rees, Peter Malsom, ?, Robert Escott, ?.

CHAPTER 4

Commercial Establishments

127. As mentioned earlier in this book, the first store belonging to the Abersychan, British and Talywain Co-operative Society was opened in Old Lion Terrace in 1889, and remained there until new premises were built in High Street in 1896. During the next five years the shop was enlarged considerably to include millinery, drapery and outfitting as seen in this 1908 photograph with the canopies extended. Elder readers will no doubt recall the 'Co-op Divi', the system of returning shop profits to the customer, the original purpose of all Co-operative stores. The tall building next to the Co-op was Witchell's boot factory which is described in the following illustration.

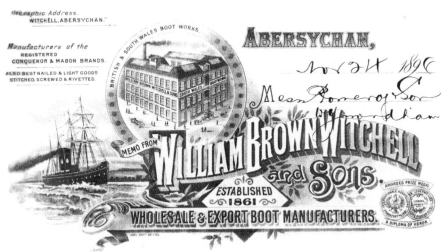

128. An early promotional letterhead from William Brown Witchell the celebrated boot manufacturer of Abersychan during the nineteenth and early twentieth centuries. Formed in 1861, the company subsequently commenced manufacture of boots and shoes in their High Street works; the family also owned a retail shop in Blaenavon. After closure as a boot factory, the building was converted into the Empire Theatre, opening in February 1910 and in later years, as the film industry developed, it became the Capitol Cinema.

129. A scene outside the new Co-op bakery in about 1912. Until 1897 when the first bakery was built in High Street, the Co-op relied on a local baker to supply their bread. However, demand gradually outstripped supply and new premises were built in about 1907, employing eight bakers and three delivery men, some of whom are seen in this photograph. Some 10,000 loaves of bread were produced and delivered each week direct to the customers' homes, the Co-op members paying by means of small metal checks rather than cash, the checks denoting the weight of the loaf required.

130. The Co-operative store as it appeared in 1939, the organisation having changed its name to the Abersychan and Pontypool Society Ltd. in June 1937.

131. This is the management committee of the Abersychan and Pontypool Co-op in 1939 and can be named as follows - Back Row: C. Cox, J. Law, Cllr. J.H. Barrett, Cllr. C. Jones and J.W. Haycock. Centre: A.S. Jones, G. Barwood, G. Reece, A.J. Rowles and R.C. Perrin Front: Mrs. E. Williams, H.D. Cotton (Gen. Manager), W.H. Blackmore J.P. (President), E. Lewis (Gen. Secretary) and E. Jones.

132. The Talywain branch of the Abersychan Co-operative Society at the junction of Commercial Road and Co-operative Terrace, was extended between 1910-1911. Part of the extension, the grocery department, is seen here in about 1913 with some members of staff. Three names have been positively identified as Mabel Harper (2nd from the left), Mabel Coleman (3rd from the left) and Bertram Harper (2nd from the right).

133. This scene at Commercial Road Talywain in about 1912 would be totally unrecognisable these days, with all of the buildings in view now demolished. The once familiar-looking branch of the Co-op was opened here in April 1908.

134. At one time, shops belonging to the Co-operative Society could be found scattered widely in the district and this is the Victoria Village branch which had opened for business in May 1911. In later years, one section of the building was converted into a private dwelling and the remainder occupied by the Abersychan and Pontypool Co-op Society. After this closed, the local Scout Movement made good use of the premises until total demolition in the early 1990s. The village could also boast another Co-op for many years, that in Harpers Road which was opened by the Garndiffaith and Varteg Industrial Provident Society in 1909; this particular building is presently a hairdressing salon.

135. High Street as already mentioned, was at one time the shopping centre of Abersychan with shops selling almost anything the inhabitants might ever need. This is the bootmaker and repair business belonging to William Weaver at Number 116 with two of his sons in the doorway. Mr. Weaver's shop was situated at the entrance to the present-day car park towards the lower end of High Street.

136. From 1908 here is just one of half a dozen butcher's shops in Abersychan at the time, this one belonging to William Hodder of 137 High Street. The name Hodder appears on several occasions within the town's business community, Obediah - a butcher in Broad Street for many years, J. & G. Hodder the jeweller's in Union Street and Wilfred Hodder who found fame on the rugby field, playing for Pontypool, winning three caps for Wales in 1921 and answering the call of rugby league.

137. Some of the few remaining houses of old Varteg which belong to Kear's Row are pictured in about 1917. To the left may be seen the former Co-op store and site of the old Varteg Brewery, whilst on the right is the Post Office after having moved from its original building in Post Office Row. The Office made a third and final move, accompanied by the Co-op, to a new location close to Salisbury Terrace, on the main road to Blaenavon and there it remained until closure in 1975.

138. Stood outside his grocery and fishmonger's shop at Number 2 Broad Street, is one of the district's longest-serving tradesmen Mr. George Parker. Mr. Parker began his business at the tender age of ten, selling fish from his basket carried from door to door before opening his Broad Street shop. He was to continue trading for an amazing 68 years before finally retiring, the Abersychan shop premises being demolished in 1999.

139. The year is 1937 and a fruit and green-grocery shop belonging to Reg Gough can be seen decorated for the coronation of King George VI in May of that year. The Gough family had shops in Broad Street and High Street Abersychan and also at Garndiffaith.

140. A scene from the 1960s, on the forecourt of Garndiffaith Garage when it was owned by the Davies family. At the time, petrol was available here for just 4/1d (20½p) per gallon and stood at the pump are Mrs. Jean Davies, Keith Prior and Mr. Glyn Davies. In 1967 the business was expanded with the opening of new premises at Cwmbran. Today, this is the well-known dealership of Newtown Motors and still a family-run concern.

141./142. Two photographs that recall the former business of Uriah Jones whose shop once stood on Stanley Road Garndiffaith and was situated where the flats are today, near the surgery. In the doorway are Mr. Jones' children Ivy, Ken and Elsie and pictured on the right is Ray Boulter who worked for Mr. Jones delivering coal. In keeping with local nicknames of course, Uriah was always known as 'Jones The Coal'.

143. A unique surviving photograph of the Black Horse Inn which once stood in Albert Road Talywain, the landlord at the time, being Mr. William Roynon. This was just one of five public houses to embellish Albert Road, the others being the Britannia, Nags Head, Railway and Albert Inn. The Black Horse later closed as a pub to be converted into a shop owned by Edward Thickpenny and subsequently demolished altogether.

144. As will be apparent in the next few pages, the district was not deprived of licensed premises in years gone by. Here is another one, the Miners Arms which stood in Union Street Abersychan and is pictured in about 1914. A local coal merchant is stood in the doorway accompanied by a young girl, Nora Gertrude Reed, daughter of landlord Evan James Reed and later to become Mrs. Boddington.

145. Another of Talywain's former 'locals' was the White Horse Inn which was situated in Commercial Road, opposite the approach road to the station. The picture, with an Austin A35 van parked alongside the pub probably dates from the early 1960s, when a pint of beer could be bought for no more than six new pence!

146. The Unicorn Inn in High Street Abersychan during the 1950s when Mr. Tibbs was 'mine host'. Situated on the corner of the lane leading to Exeter Place, the premises will be better known these days as the New Inn; the name and licence being transferred from a previous and since-demolished 'New Inn' further down the street.

147. The Hanbury Hotel as seen in 1906 when it was in the capable hands of Mr. William Ellis. The Hanbury is the sole survivor of the numerous licensed premises of Garndiffaith, with two former such establishments seen on this old picture. On the right is the White Lion and on the extreme left is the corner of the New Inn. Both of these inns were later converted into shops before being pulled down during the 1980s.

148. Another long lost 'local' is pictured here in about 1962, the popular Rose and Crown, originally known as the Crown Inn. This used to stand in Bailey Street Garndiffaith at the bottom of Butler's Lane, part of the building at one time being the grocery shop belonging to Mr. Alfred Weeks before being purchased by the brewery to enlargen their pub.

149. When it was the main thoroughfare towards Blaenavon and prior to the construction of the new road, this was a busy little corner in Cwmffrwd. The photograph from the 1930s, shows a quieter scene however, with that popular pub the Twyn-y-Ffrwd in view; the landlord at the time was Mr. Abraham George Williams.

150. The White Horse which may be remembered by some former patrons, was another popular haven in Garndiffaith and used to stand in Percy Street. As with a number of such premises, it managed to earn itself a nickname amongst the locals and this pub was often referred to as 'The Ramping Cat' or 'The Ramper'.

151. The former Greyhound Hotel situated at Number 2 Pisgah Road Talywain has changed its function more than once since this picture was taken. After closure as a hostelry, it became the home of Talywain Rugby Club in February 1972, before the members acquired their new clubhouse in Emlyn Park during the early 1980s. The Greyhound has since taken a completely new direction, it presently housing the Zion Community Fellowship.

152. The White Hart was yet another Garndiffaith public house that did not survive the demolition plans carried out in the district. This pub stood in Earl Street and can be seen here with its Hobby Horse trademark, which was acquired by the Rhymney Brewery Company and to become a distinctive part of 'pub' decor throughout South Wales.

153. The Crown Hotel which stands on the often windswept but panoramic Varteg to Blaenavon Road is seen here in about 1962. This old building is steeped in history, originally comprising of a number of small cottages dating back to the latter years of the eighteenth century. In the latter half of the nineteenth century, the premises were enlarged and converted into the hotel which remained in business until 1966. By then, the population had somewhat diminished in the area and the Crown was closed and remained in a derelict state for almost eighteen years. In 1984 however, complete rejuvenation took place thanks to the efforts of Mr. and Mrs. Rowlinson who restored this ancient building to its former eminence.

154. The closing photograph in this chapter is of The Colliers Friend, a one-time local pub in Stoney Road Garndiffaith and often referred to as 'The Stones'. Difficult to recognise these days, the premises have been completely transformed and converted into a private dwelling.

CHAPTER 5

Sports and Leisure

155. This book would not be complete without some mention of the sporting activities in the district, and here is a picture of an Abersychan rugby team from the early 1960s. The names supplied are as follows, left to right. Back: D. Leek, J. Jones, C. Oliver, K. Leek, R. Sulaway, D. Hassel and Don Brown. Middle: J. Parry, E. Pearce, C. Harding and D. Edwards. Front: A. Harris, C. Griffiths, G. Clark and L. Roynon.

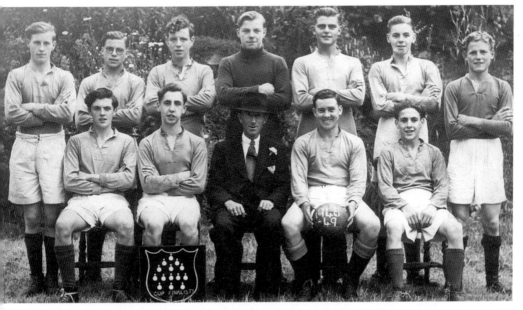

156. An Abersychan Under 18s soccer team in 1948/49 when they reached the final of the Cale and Smith Cup in Pontypool Park (unfortunately they lost to New Inn). Their ground was at the Lasgarn, close to the site of the former Isolation Hospital with changing rooms in a building behind Abersychan Police Station. Seen in this picture are - Back: K. Taylor, R. Wells, G. Hinnem, C. Cobley, M. Leighton, J. Newitt and H. Pearce. Front: C. Hurcombe, R. Touhig, Mr. Scrivens (Manager), G. Herbert and R. Hubbard.

157. Talywain R.F.C. who were winners of the Monmouthshire League and Ben Francis Cup in the 1948-49 season and runners-up the previous year. In the photograph are - Back: W. Chivers, H. Hayward, G.B. Tuckwell, D. Davies and A. Freeman. 4th Row: I. James, C. Reardon, A. Roberts, J. Davies, A. Sulway, I. Mahoney, G. Jones, J. Onions, A. Watkins and R.W. Watkins. 3rd Row: J. Gwyn (trainer), A. Waite, F. Touhig, F. Parry, G. George, S. Cobner, H. Baldwin, J. Leek, J. Evans, W. Tucker, J. Cobley, J. Hill (trainer) and W.L. Williams. 2nd Row: W.I. Tuckwell (Asst. Sec.), T. Foulke (Treas.), S. Parry, A. Parry, W.J. Rees (Pres.), W.A. Williams (Capt.), C.F. Hudson (Chair.), J. Smith, E. Thomas, W.F. Smith (Hon Sec.) and R. Edwards (Line). Front: A. Lloyd, C. Sulway, R. Parry, W.J. Curtis, D. Gould and R. Jolliffe.

158. A Talywain RFC 'Fifteen' from the mid 1960s comprises of the following players - Back: Mike Hancock, Terry Watkins, David Boddington, Graham Fry, Brian Foster, Lionel Watkins, John Parry and Neil Hancock. Centre: Ray Watkins, Mostyn Webb, Don Jenkins (Captain), Roger Pipe and Lyn Watkins. Front: Derek Flowers and Cy Morgan.

159. Garndiffaith Rugby Club members pose for a photograph with a trophy at the end of a successful 1956-57 season and the gentlemen include - Back: Jack Roberts, David Boddington, Colin Williams, John Davies, Mr. Williams, Colin Murphy and R. Dando. Centre: Ken James, Andrew Tew, Martyn Roynon, Joey Clark, Josh Parfitt (Capt.), Brian Gould, D. Smith and Tom Williams. Front: Gwillym Jones, John Bridges, Ianto Davies and J. Griffiths.

160. An earlier season at Garndiffaith R.F.C. - 1947-48 with the picture uniquely containing five sets of brothers. To be seen are - Back: C. Butcher, R. Cole, W. Weaver, W. Gauntlett, G. Scrivens, J. Randel, G. McCann, D. Davies, W. Jones and F. Parfitt. 3rd Row: A. Jeffries, J. Watkins, W. Evans, B. Parfitt, T. Cokeham, K. Carey, W. Priddle, G. Oliver, J. Gullick, E. Gullick, R. Davies and W. Tucker. Seated: T. Edwards, M. Rees, J. Scrivens, C. Reed, D. Tucker (Capt.), S. Griffiths, V. Gould, C. Harris and E. Rawlings. Front: S. James, J. Stevens, G. Webb, K. James and R. Cokeham.

161. The clock has been turned back quite some years for this Pentwyn soccer team, that year being 1926 and the players have celebrated the winning of the Ivor Jones Cup. Only a few names have been traced unfortunately and they are - Back Row: Mr. Waters and Harold Cooper (1st & 2nd left) and Ivor Morgan (6th left). Third Row: Mr. Hall (2nd left), Vic Cooper (5th left) and Sam Trollope (Far Right). Second Row: Harry Cooper (2nd left) and Jim Waters (4th left). Front: Arthur Blackmore (Right).

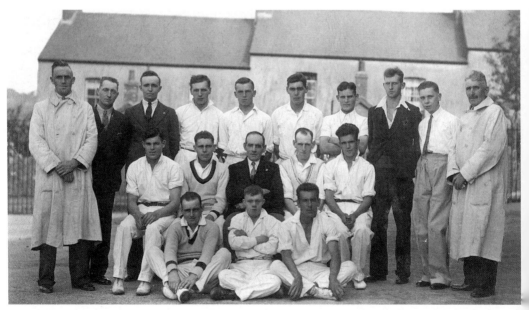

162. Another sporting team from Pentwyn and this time it's the turn of some cricketers to be photographed in the 1930s with Caradoc Street in the background. In the picture are - Back: William Law, Mr. Burlers, Arthur Davies, Jim Waters, Dick Burland, Sam Peacock, Les Handy, Sidney Beck, Rowley Cooper and Tom Deacon. Middle: George Handy, Reg Cooper, Bill Lewis, Tommy Jayne and Ivor Morgan. Front: Harry Jayne, Harold Cooper and Eddie Stone.

163. Garndiffaith A.F.C. players as they appeared in the 1948-49 season and left to right they are - Back: Roy Sullaway, Idris Randall, George Wall, Wilf White, Mr. Watkins and Eddie Britton. Middle: Wilf Jeffries, Ron Williams, Les Deacon, Arthur Waters, Haydn Jeffries, Ben Harris, Russell James, Vic Randall and Tommy Saunders. Front: Edgar Frost, George Buist, Jack Dobbs, Jack Harris, Ben Davies and Ron Dobbs.

164. Members of Garndiffaith Cricket Club in 1949 and left to right are - Back: Geth Owen, F. Coombes, J. Mann, Glyn Owen, W. Harris, T. Leonard, D. Parry, G. Jones, T. Cooper, Fred Carey, Alf Mann and Ike Chivers. Front: Tom Scull, O. Wilcox, R. Price, W. (Bruce) Harris, D. Webb and John Cole.

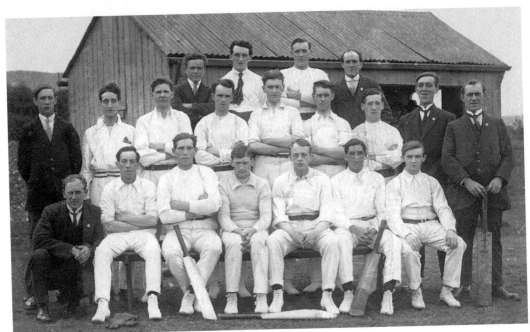

165. A Varteg 'Cricket Eleven' together with some supporters, are pictured on their ground at the old Coke Yard in about 1918. Unfortunately only one name has come to hand at the date of publication, that of Mr. William Austin Jones who is first left in the back row. Mr. Jones was responsible for marking the pitch, later graduating to play for the team.

166. Varteg A.F.C. who were Usk and District League Logan Gale Cup Winners in 1938-39 are pictured outside Varteg Institute. The gentlemen's names have been traced as follows - Back row: J. Evans, G. Bates, R. Escott, Percy Page, J. Jones, H. Carey, P. Rees (sec.), J. Jones. Middle: W. Haines (Chairman), B. Thomas (Post Office), Billy Bates, Billy Griffiths, Lyn Griffiths, Alf Edwards, S. Bryant, Y. Evans (Crown), J. Gorman, M. Millar. Front: Graham Webb, Fred Williams, Wilf Davies, Reg Pugsley, Vernon Harrison, Angus Harrison (Captain), Charlie Edwards, Billy Day, Jack Lewis, J. Shamps-Edwards.

167. An Abersychan scout group are seen during the 1930s at the rear of the White Hart Inn with some houses of Old Road in the background. A few names from the two front rows are as follows - Front: (Starting with third from the left) Tommy Hodder, George Smith, George Viner, Granville Rees, Dennis Strong, Nip Jones, Glyn Whittingham and Colin Dennis. 2nd Row: Charlie Crook, ?, Master Gough, ?, Billy Williams, Captain Evans, ?, ?, ? and Cliff Giles.

168. Members of Abersychan's British Legion Ladies' Skittles Team and catering staff display a collection of trophies during the 1960s. Standing left to right are - Ethel Roden, Doreen McCarthy, Evelyn Matthews, ?, ?, Ann Taylor, Muriel Saunders, ?, Molly Dobbs and unknown. Seated: Mrs. Perkins, Mrs. Jones, Phyllis Jones, unknown and Freda Fullard.

169. This photograph dating from the 1950s is of the darts team at the Hanbury Hotel Garndiffaith. Holding the shield is Ted Giles with 'Punchy' Clark stood at the back. Just two other names have been retrieved, Tom Weeks (landlord) holding the glass and Les Hutton to his immediate left.

170. The Pontypool and Abersychan Cage Bird Society was formed during the 1930s and this is a picture from an annual presentation which was held in the Co-op hall in High Street in about 1960. Amongst the many faces to be seen are - Mr. and Mrs. Roger Crouch, Fred Bullock, Tom Peacock, Sid Parker, Fred Dravsey, Don McVay, Tommy Guest, W.O. Smith, Mr. and Mrs. Hopkins (Abertillery), Mr. and Mrs. Ron Parfitt, Mr. and Mrs. Tommy Harper, Huw Foster, Mr. and Mrs. Cliff Robson, Mr. and Mrs. Ted Hounslow and Colin Little.

CHAPTER 6

Local People and Events

171. The war in Europe ended in May 1945 and celebrations to mark the end of six years of conflict were held nationwide. Street-dancing is in progress here at Swan Square Abersychan and the participants include Margaret Watson, Mrs. Cooper, Pam Hudson, Jean Adkins, Sheila Watson, Janet Blake, Christine Gough, Mrs. Curzon, Kate Cullis, Harold Cooper, Mrs. Smith, Mrs. Brimsdon and a young Jean Brimsdon.

172. There is probably a celebration of a kind here at the Hanbury Hotel Garndiffaith during the 1960s and the customers are Roger Tucker, David Crandon, Roger Rudge, Mr. Price, Jeff Samuel, Mike Williams, Brian Cooper and Bob Jeffries.

173. 1951 was the year of the Festival of Britain with street parties and carnivals galore held to celebrate the event. This picture shows the Victoria Village Festival Queen, Ann Kinnersley with her maids of honour. Unfortunately only two of the maids' names can be traced as Valerie Bowen (front left) and Susan Weeks (back right). The girls are also accompanied by Mr. Granville West, Member of Parliament for the constituency at the time and Mrs. West (later to become Lord and Lady).

174. Two scenes depicting a Varteg carnival during the 1960s with the parade making its way down Varteg Lane towards Garndiffaith. Local inhabitants may well remember some of the children's faces on the float belonging to Frieda Roffey's Dance Troupe and also the familiar 'Prefabs' seen in the background which have since been demolished.

175. An ensemble of local ladies pictured at the Varteg Band Hall probably during the late 1940s or early 1950s. It is believed the gentleman on the far right is Mr. Harry Wyatt and the occasion being a Christmas celebration.

176. An assembly of young lady entrants for the Garndiffaith carnival is gathered here in about 1950, when Yvonne Reid was Queen for the day and her court ladies were Susan Weeks, Yolande Forsey, Diane Luter and Valerie Bollen. Pictured left to right the girls are - Front: Myrna Martin, ?, Georgina McCann, Pat Britton, Kathleen Evans, Valerie Bollen, Pauline Courtney and Ann Pearce. 2nd Row: Pam Green, Kathleen Jones, Valerie Taylor, Joyce Williams, Audrey Horler, Diane Luter and Ann Parry. 3rd Row: Jacqueline Jones, Dorothy Thompson, Gill Malsom, Glenys Whiteman, Judith Coles and Ann George. 4th Row: Alice Jones, Isobel Parry, Wendy George, Yolande Forsey, Susan Weeks, Brenda Williams and Jean Davies. 5th Row: Pam Mark, ?, Joan Felton, ?, Ann Bridges and Ann Philpot. 6th Row: Sheila Crimmins, ?, Barbara Thomas, Yvonne Reid, Voyna Nash, Barbara Reagan and Mrs. Jones.

177. The Queen's Coronation in June 1953 was another good reason for celebration, and here are members of Frieda Roffey's Dance Troupe pictured inside the Band Hall at Varteg. Amongst the troupe are Frieda Roffey, Anita Parker, Kay Matthews, Anita Matthews, Sandra Weeks, Susan Butcher, Derek Hobbs and Roffey Edwards.

178. For today's readers of this book there may well be a grandparent on this photograph, one that was taken on a Garndiffaith Pensioners' trip to Porthcawl in the 1950s. A few names are known such as Margaret Jones, Dorothy Jones, Mr. and Mrs. Tom Bridges, Mrs. Richards, Mrs. Hopkins and Mrs. Morris.

179. The date of this photograph is January 1937 and is of an audience at a concert held in the Band Hall at Varteg. For some reason nearly all those in the picture have a rather sombre look about them, especially as it was so close to the festive season! Hopefully however, there may be a descendant of one of these residents now reading this book and able to identify a face in the crowd.

180. Royal occasions will always provide good reason for a 'street get-together' and here, residents of Pentwyn are celebrating the Queen's Silver Jubilee at Lethbridge Terrace in 1977. Standing are - Mrs. Llewellyn, an unknown lady with child, Reg Smith, Mrs. Owen, Mr. Robinson, Evelyn Smith, Stan Cook, Herbert James, Margaret James, Mr. and Mrs. Phillips, Mrs. Cooper (seated), Mrs. Denton and Bert Llewellyn. Seated at the table - Margaret Davies, Tom Davies, and Louise and Juliet Malnati.

181. The former Snatchwood Hospital which was originally the private residence of Mr. Edward Jones, the local colliery-owner and founder of an all important company, Partridge, Jones and John Paton Ltd. Edward Jones died in 1903 but his widow continued to occupy the mansion until her death in 1928. The premises later saw new usage and became attached to St. Lawrence Hospital Chepstow, as an orthopaedic recovery unit treating wounded servicemen of World War Two. Following this, it gradually converted its services into care for the elderly and geriatric patients until NHS re-organisation forced ultimate closure. The long-standing landmark at Snatchwood soon fell into disrepair and was eventually pulled down in 1992.

182. The year is about 1955 at Snatchwood and the occasion is probably the presentation of a most acceptable television set to the hospital. Matron Hiley and the chairman of Pontypool U.D.C. are either side of the T.V. and amongst the staff and guests are Elsie Purnell, Llewellyn Jones, Sister Phyllis Hill, Mr. Johnson, Mr. Smith (Head Gardener), Kay Bluett and Ivy Luxton (Cook).

183. The community spirit of Varteg is ably demonstrated here with a group photograph taken at Blackpool in 1958, a trip organised by Jim and May Williams. Not all of the trippers have been identified but here is a selection - Mr. and Mrs. Williams, Mr. and Mrs. Miller, Nora Miller, Mrs. Flook, Mrs. Weeks, Mr. and Mrs. Rowley Williams, Mr. and Mrs. Alan Jones, Mr. and Mrs. Ron Escott, Clarice Williams, Alice Giles, Mrs. Tottle, Mr. Price and Robert Escott.

184. A local grandiose wedding photograph that displays the appropriate dress-sense of eighty years ago. The occasion is the marriage of William Henry Mayers to Gertrude Hodder (daughter of Mr. and Mrs. William Hodder, High Street) at the English Baptist Church Abersychan on 12th August 1919. A few of the guests are known as follows, left to right - Back: Percy Mayers and Albert Lloyd (Nos.1 and 2) and Wilf Hodder (far right). Third Row: Sydney Gwilliam, Lillian Mayers, Kate Mayers, ?, ?, Alice Jane Mayers, ?, ?, ?. Second Row: ?, John Morris Mayers, Louisa Mayers, Wm. Henry Mayers, Gertrude Hodder, Mrs. Hodder, Mr. Hodder, ?. Front Row: ?, ?, Edna Mayers, and some additional bridesmaids Marjorie Hodder, Rene Link and Dorothy Jones.

185. The Garndiffaith and District Brass Band pose for a picture outside the Hanbury Hotel in 1911 and the musicians are as follows. Back: J. Weeks, G. Watkins, W. Bagshaw, J. Challoner, W. Parry, W. Weeks, E. Blount, H. Gascoigne, F. Giles, S. Bright and W. Jeffries. Middle: S. Miles, C.J. Ellis, T. Phelps, G. Fry, A. Fry, H. Carter (Sergeant), S. Williams, T. Barry, J. Bright and J. Gray. Front: T. Phipps, S. Hopkins, J.D. Jones D.C., J. Griffin (Bandmaster Bob), William Ellis (Landlord), H.L. Griffin and J. Johns.

186. Some local citizens are gathered here for this photograph taken in the British Community Hall. Whilst the picture is some forty years old, there are no doubt many readers of this book who will be able to remember a face or two.

187. The Varteg Silver Band, who shot to fame in September 1936 when they qualified for entry into the National Band Competition held at Crystal Palace London. Out of a total of 33 strong competitors, Varteg Band achieved third place and honour to the village. Seen in this photograph are - Back: H. Pearce, G. Wyatt, C. Morgan, W. Jones and B. Harrison. Middle: S. Jones, R. Escott, S. Morgan, J. Jones, F. Watkins, H. Malsom, A. Challenger, H. Wills, H. Rees and C. Crewe. Front: J. Knock, H. Coles, C. Coles, J. Sims, J. Tipton (Conductor), E. Coles, G. Jones, W. Hawkins and H. Jones.

188. A popular youth organisation in years past was the Boys Brigade and here are some members at Varteg during the 1930s. Back: J. Gullis, C. Wilcox, G. Webb, M. Hobbs, T. Hobbs, E. Church, B. Burkins and A. Watkins. Third Row: M. Webb, A. Challenger, W. Davies, L. Griffiths, N. Lewis, B. Bendall, F. Williams, D. Davies, H. Bryant, G. Bates, A. Jones and J. Crewe. Second Row: J. Williams, T. Bendall, A. Stockham, G. Brace, T. Davies, J. Griffiths and E. Harris. Front: B. Viner, A. Wilcox, C. Wall, D. Hawkins, L. Lewis and C. Sage.

189. Thirty-six members of the part-time Fire Brigade of Garndiffaith and District are pictured here during the 1940s. The men were stationed on the top floor of the Garndiffaith bus garage on Varteg Road and could be found doing their training at Rock Villa and the canal in Llanover. What started as an auxiliary service at the outbreak of war in 1939, was soon to become a National Fire Service, the local unit having a military 'Green Goddess' fire engine and two motorbikes at their disposal. Luckily there were no air attacks in the area requiring the officers services.

190. This is an unusual published picture postcard from about 1910 which states 'Where the remains of Edwin Pincott was discovered - Messrs Vipond's Colliery is seen in the background'. Apparently Edwin Pincott was a young boy from the Abertillery area who had wandered off whilst whinberry-picking on the mountain and became totally lost. His skeletal remains were not found for some time, until dogs belonging to a local farmer, Mr. Parker, made the gruesome discovery near Vipond's Colliery. A marker is seen on the picture indicating where the body was found.

CHAPTER 7
Industrial Times

191. The worst mining disaster ever to hit the Eastern Valley was that at Llanerch Colliery on February 6th 1890, an underground explosion claiming the lives of 176 men and boys. This particular photograph, of some rarity, was taken at the pithead and depicts those who survived the event; despite the appalling loss of life, the pit was re-opened for business shortly after on February 19th. The Abersychan area was affected dramatically with some households suffering the loss of husbands and sons. Llanerch was originally sunk in 1858 by the Ebbw Vale Company who by 1887, had sub-let it to Messrs. Partridge, Jones & Co. This continued until nationalisation in 1947, by which time the colliery had virtually outlived its usefulness and closed shortly after.

192. A fine remnant of primitive mining engineering is seen here in about 1969, Cwmbyrgwm Water Balance Pit at the British, Talywain. There were four such pits operating in this part of Talywain originally, all dating from the very early years of the nineteenth century, long before more efficient methods of winding coal to the surface were devised. The shaft is in the process of being filled in under the supervision of Mr. Thomas James Harris M.E., seen here on the right and who was a former manager at Blaensychan Colliery and later, Six Bells Abertillery.

193. Blaensychan Colliery, the closure of which on August 8th 1985 brought deep coal mining to an end in the Eastern Valley. Sunk in the year 1890 by the Partridge, Jones Co., coal was lifted to the surface until 1969-70 when it was decided to transport it underground to Hafodyrynys via Tirpentwys where, it was washed and distributed onwards by rail. In 1977 Blaensychan coal was further re-routed underground to Abertillery New Mine and finally, until its closure in 1985, the coal was raised at Marine Colliery in Cwm Ebbw Vale.

194. Provision of pithead bathing facilities at colliery workings was an unheard of luxury until the 1920s and 30s. In the background of this picture can be seen the baths which were built for the miners of Blaensychan and Llanerch. At the time, they were considered a great asset by the workers and an official opening ceremony was performed by Alderman Arthur Jenkins on May 26th 1934. Arthur Jenkins of Snatchwood, went on to become the constituency M.P.; his son Roy bringing further political acclaim to the family as a Member of Parliament, Chancellor of the Exchequer and ultimately Lord Jenkins of Hillhead.

195. Some workers are pictured at Blaensychan Colliery in about 1950, with a pithead winding wheel for background scenery and the 'boys' can be named as follows. Back Row: Jim Powell, Keith Harding, Wilf Jones, Austin Jones, Bill Howells, Deri Wall, Trevor Weeks and Len Jones. Front: Sid Hooper, Herbert Thomas, Tom Hodge, Bill Morgan, John Williams, John Waters, Watkin Jones, Tom Morgan and Jack Smithwick.

196. The steam locomotive 'Islwyn' is pictured outside the engine shed at the Big Arch in March 1970. This particular engine was built by Andrew Barclay Ltd. of Kilmarnock and originally intended for use at Lower Varteg Colliery. It began life however at Tirpentwys before later being transferred for duties between Blaensychan and Talywain. In the background may be seen striking evidence of Talywain's industrial past, the huge British tip. The three young lads on the footplate are Andrew Perry with Philip and Nigel Williams.

197. Abersychan Ironworks as they appeared in 1866. The first ironworks erected at the British were established by Messrs. Small, Shears and Taylor between 1825 and 1827, for the manufacture of merchant bars using locally mined coal and ironstone. The company was to have mixed fortunes over the years, actually running at a loss until the late 1830s before turning the corner in about 1840, when the manufacture of iron rails commenced, to meet demand from a new and rapidly expanding railway system around the country. By 1844 the company was reconstituted as the New British Iron Company which however, only lasted until 1851 when bankruptcy loomed. The Ebbw Vale Company took control in 1852 and enjoyed some measured success at the British, until the great downturn in the iron trade finally forced total closure in the early 1880s.

198. Another scene outside the Big Arch loco shed from March 1970. The engines are a former GWR pannier tank No.7754 with 'Llewellyn' manufactured by Hunslet and 'Ebbw' by Hudswell Clarke; Number 7754 was used to haul the last train, a 'Special' from Talywain to Blaensychan in 1970.

199. A unique photograph of the British Ironworks taken after final closure. The plant and machinery were sold off where possible and in 1891, demolition was undertaken by T.P.Jones and Co.of Newport. Most of the structure was pulled down with the exception of a few buildings, parts of which still stand today. Surviving remains include a Cornish beam house which was used as a pumping station, the remnants of a puddling furnace and part of an old furnace retaining wall, damaged coke ovens and some office buildings.

200./201. Both of these pictures were taken at another of the district's coal workings, Lower Varteg Slope near Garndiffaith. In the lower photograph men are seen at the slope's entrance, which has the year 1899 engraved in its stonework. This was the year when the first sod was cut by Mrs. Deakin, wife of Thomas H. Deakin managing director of the Lower Varteg Colliery Co; that undertaking being in operation some twenty years-plus before the slope. Henry Jayne, who had been associated with John Vipond for many years, re-modelled the Lower Varteg in 1898 when he assumed control of the pit in conjunction with Mr. Deakin.

202. Early methods of raising coal to the surface involved the sinking of relatively shallow shafts known as 'balance pits'. These operated on a two-cage system whereby one cage would contain a tram of coal and the other a tank of water. The tank was filled or emptied as required and so the force of gravity did the rest; such a system was used at Garndiffaith, the site of which is seen here in 1938. In the centre of the picture are Balance Houses and on the right, the remains of a shaft; the building on the left was used for stabling the horses in use at nearby Lower Varteg Colliery. The only evidence remaining at this site today is the pond which supplied water to the lifting system.

203. The area surrounding Varteg was once a plethora of coal mining activity and here is yet another such workplace, Top Pits. One of the great pioneers in the district was John Vipond, a native of Cheshire, who, having gained experience in the Midlands' coalfield, came to Monmouthshire in the 1840s. His name and efforts in the establishment of the coal industry in this part of the Eastern Valley were second to none. This early workaholic was known to rise at 4am each day and work late into the evening without fail. Sadly he paid a price, working himself into an early grave at the age of 59 in 1865, with most of the financial rewards going to his heirs.

204. Varteg Incline, which was built in the 1850s to convey coal from the Varteg collieries to the valley bottom at Cwmavon, where it connected with the newly constructed Pontypool to Blaenavon railway line. The incline was operated by means of a stationary steam engine which allowed the full wagons to be lowered and the empties raised; the passing point was just below the road bridge at the top of the picture. A large wall was later built at the bottom to stop any runaway wagons which had, on occasions, been a problem.

205. From the bottom of High Street Garndiffaith can be seen more evidence of an industrial heritage. In the background are the former waste tips belonging to Lower Varteg Colliery, which thankfully have since been removed, the land gradually returning to its natural appearance.

206. A further industrial scene from years gone by is of Navigation Colliery at the British, Talywain. Owned by the Powell Tillery Steam Coal Co., the pit was sunk between 1910 and 1912, the first coal being brought to the surface in 1913 amidst great excitement. There was however further local 'excitement' when the gentleman who sank the pit, master-sinker Mr. Jack Tintern, was convicted of shooting his wife. For the period, the sentence of a few years in prison was lenient, the mitigation being that his wife had incited the fatal argument in the first instance, a claim that was met with strong support by the local population. Consequently, on his release from prison, there were cheering and welcoming crowds of well-wishers gathered outside his home in Monmouth Row. The pit however had a relatively short life, production ceasing after the General Strike of 1926 although it did see use as a pumping station until the 1960s.

207. Prior to the arrival of the 'Industrial Revolution', the farming industry was an all-important part of valley life. This is the ancient Gelli Rhwy Farm at Garndiffaith, which is one of the oldest buildings still standing in the district of Abersychan. Once part of the Pontypool Park Estate, the building today has received some twentieth-century modernisation to its appearance.

208. Once referred to as Emlyn Road, and nowadays re-named New Road Talywain, this is the scene in about 1920; the picture providing a further example of the area's rich industrial history. In the background is John Paton's ballast-crusher works which were established in the early 1900s and where today, may be found the local rugby ground. The ballast, retrieved from the local vicinity, was transported by tramway, crushed into fine pieces and used in the construction of roads etc. Larger and uncrushed material was carried by an overhead conveyor seen here, crossing the roadway, and deposited on the ash tip. Close to the crusher was the site of the earlier Golynos Ironworks, which served the area from about 1837 until closure in 1867.

209. An industrial landmark to be remembered in Abersychan was the old gasometer which overlooked the river Avon Llwyd; used for the storage of coal-produced gas, it is seen here in about 1963. By the early 1950s however, its usefulness was on the decline, due to a new and much larger works built at New Inn with the capacity to extensively supply the Eastern Valley.

Railway Memories

210. The 'up' platform and booking office of the former GWR Abersychan Low Level station in 1908. The Eastern Valley railway line was opened from Newport to Pontypool in 1852 by the Monmouthshire Railway and Canal Company and, by 1854, the line was extended as far as Blaenavon, thereby providing the residents of Abersychan with rail travel for the first time. Abersychan also had its own goods yard which was about 100 metres south of the station, this facility closing in July 1957. Rail services lasted for more than a century in the valley before the lines north of Pontnewynydd eventually closed in April 1962.

211. Abersychan station again, this time looking south and showing the staggered-platform arrangement. In comparison with the previous photograph, it can now be seen that a footbridge has been added for passenger safety, where previously it had been necessary to walk across the lines. This particular photograph was taken from the driver's compartment of a diesel multiple unit on its way to Newport in April 1962, two weeks before closure of the service.

212. The scene is at Cwmffrwd Halt and shows rail motor car No.89 - the 'Coffee Pot Train', and the handing over of the staff to enable the train to travel onwards up the single track to Blaenavon. The nickname 'Coffee Pot' was given due to the train's unique design, whereby a central boiler system provided the necessary steam power to drive the coaches. Number 89 was allocated to Pontypool Road depot by the GWR during the years 1912-14, and these trains were extremely popular with the travelling public, so much so that on the opening Saturday alone, more than 3,000 passengers used the service.

213. The next stop up the valley after Cwmffrwd was at Cwmavon, the line now having changed to a single track. This tiny station was downgraded to a 'Halt' in 1953 and the picture from June 1957, shows a pannier tank engine No.5752 with two coaches ready for the journey to Newport.

214. Some railway staff pictured at Cwmffrwd Junction outside the early ground frame signal box in about 1913. Situated on the low level line in the Eastern Valley, the Great Western Railway Company opened a halt at Cwmffrwd in 1912; it incorporating two platforms, both constructed of timber with pagoda-design waiting rooms.

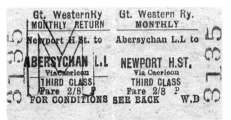

215. A much later photograph of Cwmffrwd Halt taken in 1962 and the old ground level signal box has been replaced with a much taller structure. This enabled the signalman to receive the token from the driver of the down train without having to leave his box duties. The token was a vital piece of equipment which was exchanged between the train driver and the signalmen at Cwmffrwd and Blaenavon on every journey. This was a fail-safe method of signal and points' control between the two stations, the line changing to a single track at Cwmffrwd and continuing as such, as far as Blaenavon Low Level.

216. Pictured some forty years after its opening in 1878, this is the station at Talywain which was situated on the Eastern Valley high level line. Named 'Abersychan and Talywain', it was jointly owned by the London and North Western Railway whose line from Brynmawr met with that of the Great Western from Pontypool. Although closed to passenger traffic in May 1941, the station remained open for general freight use until 1965, whilst the very last train to travel over the branch was a 'Big Pit Special' on October 30th 1982.

217. The 'Crossing Talywain', where the important Golynos Junction signal box was responsible for controlling rail traffic movements over the level crossing from Cwmffrwd Sidings, Garndiffaith Junction and the branch to the right of the picture. The old British Ironworks also made good use of this junction as did traffic from the National Coal Board in later years, until the box finally closed in June 1965.

218. A superb photograph taken at Talywain Station in the year 1906 with the arrival of a passenger train from Brynmawr. The train is headed by a 0-6-2 locomotive coal tank No.1005 owned by the LNWR and based at Abergavenny, as confirmed by the number 31, the applied shed code seen at the rear of the driver's cab. This picture was taken some ten years before photograph number 216 as the footbridge has yet to be built.

219. For many, much of the joy of train spotting waned with the passing of the steam age, however, to some, this is still an interesting photograph. Taken at Talywain in about 1970, it shows a diesel Class 37 No.6922 manufactured by English Electric, hauling wagons from Big Pit at Blaenavon which was still extracting coal at the time.

220. Driver Arthur Evans and latcher Jim Peacock are seen in the cab of this loco. They are about to pass beneath the Big Arch and ascend the bank at the rear of the once 'Brickyard Row' on the journey to the exchange sidings at Talywain in 1970.

221. Varteg Station with its substantial building and single platform is seen here in 1906 whilst Mr. Charles Chivers was the stationmaster in charge. Although closed in 1941, the station house was occupied for quite a number of years thereafter until the eventual demolition.

222. The final photograph in this book looks northwards along Varteg Station towards Blaenavon from the Snailcreep bridge. In 'the good old days' passengers wishing to travel from Brynmawr to Newport had a choice of routes; they could either travel down the Western Valley line through Abertillery and Crumlin etc. or the Eastern, which took them through Blaenavon, Varteg and so on. Either way, the journey would have been a most interesting and enjoyable experience, a far cry perhaps from that same journey if it were made today in the absence of any railway service.

Acknowledgements

The authors are most grateful to the undermentioned who kindly loaned some of thei original material and valuable time for the production of this book. Sincere apologies ar extended to anyone who may have been inadvertently omitted due to an unintende oversight.

Mr. Roger Appleby, Mr. Louis Bannon, Mr. Jeffrey Bird, Mr. & Mrs. David Boddington, M & Mrs. G. Boulter, Mrs. Irene Boulter, Mr. Brimsdon, Mr. Don Britton, Mrs. D. Butcher, Mrs May Clark, Mr. John Coles, Mr. Reg Cooper, Mr. & Mrs. Caleb Counsell, Mr. Barry Davies Mr. Glyn Davies, Mr. Gerald Davies, Mr. Ron Dobbs, Mr. Ken Forward, Mrs. Bessie Harding Mr. Bev Harris, Mrs. Gill Harris, Mrs. Ann Hodder, Mr. & Mrs. Ted Hounslow, Mr. C Herbert, Mr. & Mrs. M. Jennings, Mrs. Elsie Jones, Mrs. Beatrice Jones, Mr. & Mrs. Terr Jones, Mr. Graham Jones, Mr. Derek Keenan, Mr. Bryan Mahoney, Mrs. Ruth Matthews, M Phillip Mayers, Mrs. Rita Morgan, Mr. & Mrs. Derek Parry, Mrs. Marie Rees, Mrs. Marg Roberts, Mrs. Margaret Roden, Mr. Richard Roynon, Mr. & Mrs. Reg Smith, Mrs. Susa Shrigley, Mrs. Elaine Sloman, Mrs. Joan Thomas, Mrs. Eileen Thomas, Mrs. Tyler, Mrs Judith Warmsley, Mr. Keith Watkins, Mr. Len Waters, Mrs. Mary Wilcox, Mrs. Iris Williams Mr. John S. Williams.